Eloquence:

Public Speaking Skills for Lawyers and Other Professionals

Rohan G. Bansie

Copyright © 2014 Rohan Bansie

All rights reserved. No part of this book may be used or reproduced by any means, graphic, electronic, or mechanical, whatsoever, including photocopying, recording, taping, or by any information storage retrieval system without the written permission of the author.

Published by Rohan Bansie, Ottawa.

Bansie, Rohan G. -
 Eloquence: Public Speaking Skills for Lawyers and Other Professionals / Rohan G. Bansie

ISBN 978-0-9937798-0-0

Edited by Jasmine Ball

Cover Art by Jasmine Ball
Author portrait by Patrick Blake Photography

Table of Contents

Introduction   9

Chapter 1.   Make the Commitment: The First Step to Becoming an Effective Communicator   15

Chapter 2.   We're All Salespeople: Selling Your Ideas to an Audience   25

Chapter 3.   Non-verbal Communication: Improving Your Image in the Role of Advocate   35

Chapter 4.   Creating a Dialogue: Communicating with Your Audience   41

Chapter 5.   Dynamic Descriptions: Connecting to Your Audience Through Storytelling   49

Chapter 6.   Presentation Elements: Presenting to a Jury   57

Chapter 7.   Organizing Your Argument: The Mechanics of Effective Submissions   63

Chapter 8.   The Fear Factor: Overcoming Public Speaking Anxiety   71

Chapter 9.   Your Reaction Matters: Receiving the Verdict   81

Afterword   83

*Dedicated to the memory of:
my grandmother, Matilda Hyman;
my parents, George and Rema Bansie;
and my Grade 7 teacher, Mrs. Joyce Cloutier.*

INTRODUCTION

If you are a lawyer, or are studying to become one, there is no doubt that you are academically adept. Everyone who gets accepted into and completes law school knows how to succeed academically. But the truth is when you get to Court, no one's looking at your transcript. The only thing that matters in that position is how well you advocate on behalf of your client. There is an art to it. There are expected codes of conduct and appropriate addresses. There are effective ways to present an argument and practical skills of persuasion. There is skill in reading body language and modifying your delivery to better align with your audience (the judge and/or jury). And, most critically, there is a way to accomplish your goal of presenting a strong case persuasively while respecting the Court. Demonstrating and earning respect is fundamental in order to communicate well. Without respect, you cannot control your message or how it is perceived.

The fact that you've picked up this book bodes well for you. You have demonstrated an interest in personal growth and in gaining a better understanding of yourself and others, which will help you on your quest to become an eloquent advocate. But who am I to be dispensing advice?

I am a lawyer and mediator with a B.A. (philosophy) from Concordia and an M.Ed. (psychology) and LL.B. /J.D. from the University of Ottawa. My current practice is focused on insurance and civil litigation, and previously included personal injury litigation, commercial litigation, and sports and entertainment law. I have experience before all levels of courts in the Province of Ontario, including the Court of Appeal.

Prior to becoming a lawyer, mediator and eventually a judge, I had a successful career in training and development/management consulting and teaching. The focus of my consulting activity was in coaching, staff and individual motivation, addressing change and time management issues, and the development and delivery of training programs.

I am a trained mediator with over 25 years of experience in assisting clients with conflict resolution issues and have been appointed to the roster of court-connected mediators in the Ontario Superior Court.

I have provided lectures and workshops on various topics of law, as well as advocacy, litigation, and negotiations. I have also lectured to law students, lawyers, paralegals, and articling students as part of ongoing continuing legal education commitments for lawyers and paralegals in Ontario.

In 2007, I was appointed as Deputy Judge of the Superior Court of Justice, Small Claims Court.

Being an effective communicator has helped me succeed in all areas of my life. I have always admired people who spoke well. When I was a child, that meant the televangelists who delivered Sunday programs and the preachers at my family's church. These were charismatic storytellers and they had a knack for making the stories they shared truly riveting. Growing up in the midst of the turmoil of the 60s and 70s, there were also many notable speeches that were televised. I noticed that the politicians and activists who spoke to audiences of thousands commanded the attention and captured the imagination of their audiences. As I grew older I came to see the same characteristics in comedians, and all I could think is that I wanted to be able to speak like these public speakers – with charisma, poise, and personality.

I consumed multiple resources about effective communication in an effort to discover what made good communicators good. But I realized that, as an introvert, I had to take a different approach to communicating well. Introversion and extroversion have become common cultural terms, and each has a number of stereotypes attached to the term. But at the most basic level, people with these personality types differ in the manner in which they acquire their energy. The difference is in the amount of outside stimulation each type requires in order to function optimally. Psychiatrist Carl Jung popularized the terms introvert and extravert (now commonly spelled 'extrovert') in his 1921 book, *Psychological Types*, explaining their relations to external stimuli and positioning these attributes as core personality traits. In this work, Jung posited that people who are most charged by solitary pursuits demonstrate a preference for introversion and those who are enlivened by external stimuli, like social interaction, are extroverts. Introverts and extroverts each have their own strengths and face their own struggles: the introvert might excel at performing research but, due to a naturally withdrawn personality, might not be able to deliver it eloquently; on the other hand, the extrovert might win over an audience easily but might struggle with one-on-one encounters due to a desire to speak rather than listen or a proneness to distraction. Introverts also tend to be more deliberate in their actions and can operate best without external stimulants or distractions. They are happy to immerse themselves in their work. Extroverts are more likely to jump right into an assignment and be more daring in their approach. They shine when they are engaged in group activities, such as chairing meetings. There are elements to every person's work that might be more challenging, regardless of their personality type. But both introverts and extroverts can learn to communicate more effectively, especially in a profession that demands shrewdness in every interaction.

In my interactions, I knew well enough to reach into my toolkit to communicate effectively; I want to share that toolkit with you, whether you identify as an introvert or an extrovert. I want to provide you with tips to help you connect with people and deliver your message effectively, because I recognize that preparation is key. And once you know how to communicate well, you will find that opportunities will open to you.

Communication – and especially persuasion – is a skill that can be learned, but it is one that many people neglect to master. Learning how to effectively influence others' thoughts, beliefs, and actions will put you ahead of the pack. I wish you the best of luck on your journey to becoming a strong communicator and eloquent advocate.

CHAPTER 1

MAKE THE COMMITMENT:

THE FIRST STEP TO BECOMING AN EFFECTIVE COMMUNICATOR

While each of us has particular personality traits that determine the way we naturally interact with others, the keys to communicating effectively can be learned regardless of our preferences and challenges. There is no doubt that communicating well is a desirable skill – effective communication can increase your productivity, enrich your relationships, and enable you to have an impact on the lives of others and on the world around you – but it is especially relevant to the successful practice of law. In the legal profession, ideas and positions must be communicated clearly to everyone from clients, to opponents, to judges, to juries.

One incredibly innovative man, Dr. Larry

Richard, has made it his life's work to help legal professionals assess personality differences within firms and use that knowledge to help law firms manage their staff and operate efficiently. One tool has been especially useful to Dr. Richards. The Myers-Brigg Type Indicator (MBTI) questionnaire was developed from psychiatrist Carl Jung's theory that people could be grouped into certain personality types, and the assessment test has since been used to help people identify their preferences and determine how they make decisions as a means to promote better communication between differing personality types. Using the MBTI personality assessment, Dr. Richards has found that the legal profession tends to attract a particular group of personality types (in fact, by his calculations, more than half of all lawyers fit within only four psychological types). Given that so many within the profession think alike, lawyers risk making the mistake of assuming everyone they come into contact with will see things the way they do. This is an obstacle many lawyers have to overcome.

The truth is we all must learn to alter our communication styles to accommodate our audiences. When you are able to communicate effectively, you can have an amazing power with people. You can make things happen. Think for a minute about some of the stirring speeches delivered by Winston Churchill, John F. Kennedy or Martin Luther King Jr. Each of those great communicators shared a set of character traits and public speaking skills. Accordingly, they were able to communicate with power. Their words inspired thousands and affected the course of history. You may believe that great communicators have rare talents – that they're somehow superior to you and me – but the fact is most of them were not born with an ability to influence their audiences. They cultivated the art of communicating eloquently and they understood that they needed to put in the work to get their desired results.

Anyone can become an effective communicator. If you think you face a major obstacle to communicating well, don't accept defeat. You can absolutely improve and build upon your existing communication skills if you are willing to invest some time and practice in developing the appropriate skills. Take Winston Churchill for example. Many recognize that the Prime Minister held the United Kingdom together during the Nazi blitz of World War II, but what is not commonly known is that he had a severe speech impediment and required extensive speech therapy during his childhood and early adult years. He overcame what many would consider an insurmountable barrier to leadership, and in turn led a nation through one of its worst times in history.

Speech impediment, difficulty communicating with different personalities, stage fright; whatever afflicts you, you can become more effective at communicating. We can all reap the rewards in our careers if we manage our interactions well. It is indisputable that effective communicators are much more successful than people who have problems getting their ideas across.

I already know you are a good student, because you are studying or have studied law. So use your skill as a student to your advantage! Study other lawyers! When someone uses a key phrase effectively, write it down! If you notice that someone has won over her audience, take note! What is her demeanor? How did she handle questions or objections? In law school and during my term of articles, I studied the nuances and mannerisms of every lawyer I saw in court. I had a yellow pad of paper in which I kept meticulous notes about the tools effective speakers employed. I would sit in the back of the Courtroom and write exactly what they said. One lawyer I studied would get the judge on side by referencing the judge's knowledge. He would start by saying, "As your honour knows, in this circumstance the test is…" and then demonstrate how his argument and evidence fit within those confines. By presenting in this way, his position appeared to be indisputable so the judge would often have no choice but to rule in his favour.

It's also helpful to keep records of what not to do. Be observant. If a lawyer frustrates a judge, write down what happened. Figure out what the judge didn't like. Did the lawyer interrupt the judge, cutting him off? I learned, this way, that it is best to shut up when the judge is writing. If the judge is writing, it must be something important; so don't interrupt that thought.

Given that you are a good student, there's a good chance you are also a proficient writer. Studying lawyers are given plenty of opportunity to improve their writing skills, and there are certain conventions to drafting legal documents, in order to prevent misinterpretation or possible loopholes, that are embedded in lawyers' brains. But there are few opportunities to improve one's public speaking ability. Writers don't often get the chance to see their readers. But when speaking, you will receive constant feedback from those listening to your argument. This might seem intimidating, but it is actually a fantastic opportunity! You can survey your audience to see if people are showing an interest in what you are saying. And, if they are not, you can adjust your message or delivery to regain their interest. But you must recognize that a different medium will require a different delivery style. Readers are able to process your argument selectively. They can choose to reread certain sections and scan over others in order to gain an understanding. Your listeners, on the other hand, will not have this luxury, so you will have to do the highlighting for them. You might find that you need to repeat key points more frequently and pause to give your listeners time to process important information. The two acts require completely different skill sets, so don't expect your writing skills to transfer effortlessly into speaking ability. This book will provide you with some tools to improve your speaking skills so that you can speak with as much confidence as you write.

So are you ready to build that skill set? Before we begin, there are five conditions that you must meet if you wish to become a truly effective communicator:

1. **YOU MUST HAVE A BURNING DESIRE TO IMPROVE.**
   Humans have almost unlimited potential. We can achieve virtually anything we wish if we desire it strongly enough, but without the will there can be no true progress. Someone who desires something will commit the time and energy needed to achieve a goal. People sometimes say to me, after I've given a keynote speech or conducted a seminar, "I would give anything to be able to speak to an audience as well as you do," and my usual reply is, "You'd likely be better than I am if you invested only half the time to prepare as I have."
   The ancient Greeks lived in the golden age of

orators, in a society in which all major disputes were settled by public oration. Once there was a young man who asked to speak to the assembly and was granted a hearing on a vital issue. As he stood in front of the crowd, his weak voice trembled and his ideas were muddled. He became more anxious and less competent as the speech dragged on. Finally, his audience could stand no more. Boos and hisses forced him to step down. Humiliated, he completely withdrew from public life, but he was not so easily defeated. His humiliation gave way to a burning desire to become a great orator. He wanted to speak in a way that would move people to action. So, to improve his diction, he practiced enunciating for hours on end with stones in his mouth; to strengthen his weak voice, he shouted relentlessly into the heavy winds coming off the Aegean Sea; to clarify his presentation, he studied the techniques of the masters; and to overcome his fears, he practiced speaking with a sword hanging over his head.

When his next opportunity to speak arose years later, he was ready. He stepped in front of the assembly to warn the nation of the tremendous threat posed by Philip the Second of Macedonia. He set about to offer practical ideas on how to combat this treacherous intruder. His speech was powerful, his thoughts were clear, and his delivery was dynamic. As the echo of his final words faded, the entire audience rose as one person and began to shout, "Let us go fight Philip!" He was able to rally his fellow citizens because he had a burning desire to communicate well and get results.

2. Understand that communicating is about sending and receiving images.

We may speak in words, but we think in images. If I say the word "horse," what comes to mind? It isn't the letters H-O-R-S-E. You'll have formed a mental picture of the four-legged animal. I like to think of communicating as mind to mind reorientation. In other words, when you communicate effectively, you can change the way people think, feel and act by enabling them to understand the way you think, feel and act. A good listener can comprehend a speaker's thought process and argument by seeing things through the speaker's eyes. As a person delivering a message, it is your task to make your thinking clear to your listener. Words are only one of the vehicles we use to communicate images to each other. We also rely on such tools as pictures, sounds and gestures. We use images, whether we are trying to catch a waiter's attention to order another cup of coffee, or explaining Einstein's theory of relativity to a group of students. Humans naturally use our hands when speaking, but doing so can be distracting, so make sure that when you gesticulate your gestures are helping to paint a picture for your audience.

To communicate effectively, we must send accurate images to others, as well as receive accurate images from them. The challenge is conveying images exactly as you see them, and receiving them exactly as others see them. Make your audience see what you see.

3. Know that you do not need to be a master to begin.

There are literally thousands of books on communication that focus on the mechanics of communicating. They talk about building a large vocabulary, about learning how to structure sentences, about voice-modulation and so on. These facets of communication are important. But if you wait until you have mastered all these skills, it would be years before you could make any real progress toward becoming an effective communicator. However, you can make a start once you understand that effective communication can be broken into three basic skills:
- Connecting with an audience
- Conveying messages in terms your audience can understand
- Checking your audience's response

4. Be willing to spend the necessary time practicing.

There's an old story about a young musician who once questioned an old master. This young man approached the accomplished master, who had just moved thousands of people to tears with a magnificent rendition of a great composition. The young man said, "Sir, it must be great to have all the practicing behind you and be able to simply sit down and play like that."

"Oh," the master replied, "I still practice eight hours every day."

"But why? You're so good," exclaimed the young musician. To that, the master replied, "But I wish to become superb."

So, if you want to become a master communicator,

practice, practice, and then practice some more.

5. **BE PERSISTENT.**
As with all things, it takes time to become an effective communicator. Even if you work as hard as you can, learn as many communication techniques as you can, and practice for hours on end, mastering the skill of communicating effectively still takes time and persistence. And it takes patience to wait for the skills you acquire to mature. To become competent communicators, we must be willing to subject ourselves to constant and ruthless self-evaluation. The most hindering thought we can harbour is not "I'm doing it wrong," but, "I'm doing it right."

Whenever I teach, before I get in front of the classroom, I'm still a nervous wreck. Even after years of practice, it can take me 10 to 15 minutes to get into stride. But I've learned how to be a compelling speaker. I grow more animated, sprinkle in some humour, and move more freely as the lesson wears on. And I'm always monitoring my audience for feedback. If I'm giving a presentation and say something that elicits laughter, I'll take note of it and endeavour to create a similar response in other speaking engagements. I've learned to assess myself constantly, so I know that the next time I present I need to intentionally include segments that have been well received, and doing so makes me a better communicator with each presentation.

The same rule applies when our communication attempts fail. We must not only be willing to admit that they have failed; we must be willing to find out why they failed. There is no shame in failing. The only shame is in not learning from your setbacks. A thin line divides destructive self-criticism and constructive self-criticism. One destroys self-confidence; while the other spurs you on to try harder. Each of us must find that line for ourselves, and endeavour to use our mistakes as building blocks.

So, if you are prepared to accept these five conditions, we are ready to begin.

CHAPTER 2

WE'RE ALL SALESPEOPLE:

SELLING YOUR IDEAS TO AN AUDIENCE

Before becoming a lawyer, I spent some time working in sales. I sold everything from fitness memberships to international private banking services, and I got to be good at it. People were always trying to hire me to do sales jobs. They wanted me to sell insurance, investments, and cars. But being good at sales isn't about hustling someone. Slick salespeople might occasionally convince customers with their smooth talk and false claims, but you'll find that those who are most successful in sales and have customers return to them are those who hold a deep understanding of what a person needs and are able to address those needs. I was trained in sales on the client-based selling model, and it taught me a lot about communicating effectively.

One of the first things we need to understand

about influence and persuasion is that these aren't tasks we can simply perform. Your audience will decide whether or not you will influence them depending on how credible you appear. The soundness of an argument is determined by the person who's being persuaded. Knowing this will help you shift your communication from being persuasion technique oriented to personal transformation oriented, which has the main goal of benefiting your listener. And speaking to meet your listener's needs is one of the keys to selling.

Every single day of our lives, in the majority of the communicating we do, we are trying to influence and persuade others. We are all engaged in selling: we sell another person on our idea; sell our friends or co-workers on where to go for lunch; sell ourselves as a potential partner to someone we are attracted to. This act of selling extends to the Courtroom. A lawyer is tasked with the challenge of selling a client's position.

A lawyer advocating on behalf of his client needs to be able to connect to the judge or jury in a professional, compelling, and clear way. The audience has to be ready to buy what the lawyer is selling. If you wish to master the art of persuasion and be a person who others listen to, you will need to master your delivery of a couple of attributes.

The first is character and the second is language. Communication isn't just what you say; it's also how you perform. As my granny and mother always used to remind me, "It's not what you say and do; it's how you say and do it."

CHARACTER: This includes perceivable traits such as your attitude and your integrity.

People make decisions about whether or not they will be motivated by your pitch based on how trustworthy and competent you appear. The classic example is the car salesman. If buyers don't believe in his integrity, or don't like his attitude, they will not feel comfortable making a purchase from him; consequently, he won't be able to persuade them to make a car purchase. Even if he has the best, most cost-effective car for his customers' needs and lifestyle, he will not make the sale. Clearly, character has a big part to play even at the most superficial level. Realistically people don't walk into a car dealership and, within three minutes, think they know the depth of a salesman's character. But we all make immediate impressions on people, and others will make judgements about us within seconds.

People you try to persuade will watch you for hints of your character. They'll take note of whether you make eye-contact because in our culture we're taught that those who avert one's gaze are deemed to be untrustworthy. Your audience is wondering what kind of person you are and deciding whether you can be trusted. As a lawyer, gaining your audience's trust is essential, and this need to communicate trustworthiness will extend to your clients. Make every effort to personalize your clients. Use their names. Share a little bit of background information when presenting their cases.

Extroverts often excel in the area of client retention. Their sociable nature is attractive to clients and helps them exude confidence. But they must take care not to dominate conversations. Clients will not feel at ease if they don't feel their needs have been heard. Introverts can do well in intimate gatherings of just a few people; the struggle will likely come in establishing rapport. Introverts can draw confidence from their knowledge of a case and the law; their comfort with the material will carry over into their conversational style.

Regardless of your nature, your arguments and requests must not come across as too self-serving or your audience will grow skeptical of everything you say. Demonstrate integrity by supporting the facts. Know your case.

LANGUAGE: Through language we transmit.

Let's return to the car salesman example. In order to make sales, he's going to want to know everything there is about the cars on his lot and about cars in general, in order to project confidence in his knowledge and demonstrate his ability to carry out the functions of his job. The same is true of the legal profession. Using appropriate language helps us communicate our knowledge.

Aside from speaking the language of the profession with competence, you will need to speak well. If you wish to come across as knowledgeable and articulate, you will find that clearly enunciating your words will make an incredible impact in exchange for little effort. When you pronounce your words crisply and avoid running them together you will sound more intelligent and credible. Managing your tone and pace will also help to improve your image. Most people speak faster when speaking publicly, which can give listeners the impression of nervousness or low confidence. When you speak more slowly you will come across as more authoritative. Speaking more slowly has the added benefit of giving your audience more time to process your message. Practice inserting a two-second pause at the end of each statement to take advantage of this effect. At first it will feel painfully long, but in truth you will sound quite natural.

Most people can also stand to speak a little louder. Often the fear of overwhelming our listeners holds us back but, unless you have been told that you speak too loudly, there is a good chance you would benefit from raising your volume. Doing so will also engage your diaphragm, which will help to improve your tone of voice. Otherwise you might end up squeaking out strangled high notes as we've all heard from nervous speakers.

Once you have played with voice projection and articulation, you can work on building a broader vocabulary so you will be able to call upon the choicest words to better convey your message. When we use language well, others are more apt to be influenced by us because we will have better communicated our message and sold our perspective. Make an effort to build your vocabulary. Often when you learn a new word you'll excitedly think, "I have to start using that word!" But if the opportunity doesn't arise, soon enough you'll forget the word and rely on your usual expressions. To combat this, try using the word in a sentence right away. Get used to the feel of it. Substitute it for a word you use more commonly. Sometimes fear of judgement will hold you back from trying out an uncommon word. You may avoid using words that are so big that people will be left wondering what it means, or even thinking, "Who is he trying to impress?" And that is a valid concern, but please don't give up. If you are concerned, refer to a thesaurus to find a more audience-friendly word to use in its place. You will find that there are many great words that will strike a balance between average and ostentatious. A good communicator will consciously choose words that are appropriate for the audience. As you expand your vocabulary, you will learn to communicate in a way that will convey your messages more clearly. You will discover words that land on the perfect meaning and that lend eloquence, some panache, and some pizzazz to your speech. And people will better remember what you say as a result.

There is a plethora of words available that will add some style and flair to your sentences. For example, rather than saying, "Those products are everywhere," you can try, "Those products are ubiquitous." Drawing from a wider vocabulary will make your words memorable.

While you are practicing using more formal language, do away with the "um," "you know," "like," fillers common in informal speech. If you are to speak with force, you must also eliminate qualifiers that minimize your statements. Pause, instead, to call upon the next appropriate word.

> **WORDS TO AVOID:**
> Um, uh
> You know
> Like
> Anyway
> Et cetera
> Just
> I mean
> I feel, I believe
> Kind of, sort of
> Actually
> Basically

As you practice improving your speech, you will inevitably slip up and mispronounce a word or use a filler word you are working hard to avoid. Try not to beat yourself up over it. If you make a mistake, correct it swiftly and move on. If you fixate on it or visibly chastise yourself for your error, you will only call more attention to your mistake. Remember that slip ups are a regular part of communication. No one will think any less of you for the occasional blunder. It can be helpful to practice improving the language you use in all social interactions in order to get into the habit of speaking well. Doing so will help you avoid slipping into using language mistakes commonly used in casual interactions, as you will not have to make an additional effort when speaking more formally.

People who master influence are people who win in life. The people who rise to the high levels are those who have understood the significance and power of influence. I truly believe that the foundation for success in life is based on the ability to sell. Life is full of sales opportunities. A man has to sell himself as an attractive potential husband when he asks a girl to marry him. A homebuyer needs to master communication skills to influence and persuade the banker to give her a loan so she can buy her first house. It goes on and on and on. Our level of success in life depends on our ability to master communication skills to influence and persuade others. With this in mind, we must take advantage of every opportunity to improve our strength in communication. Remember that before we even develop an argument we influence and persuade others by establishing a foundation of character and by mastering our language.

Playing the Part

As a lawyer, before you even get to Court, you are selling on behalf of your client. For example an insurance lawyer at a settlement negotiation has to sell his evidence to the opposing lawyer and have the opposition believe in the soundness of his statements. After performing his research, he must present in a way that isn't confrontational or truculent. You don't want to do anything that would discourage your audience from liking or trusting you because it will put off your audience and reflect badly on you and your client. You want to be believable, you want to be trusted, and, believe it or not, you want to be liked.

When I'm sitting as Deputy Judge, during settlement conferences when I'm essentially mediating cases, I see it is my job to sell both parties on a settlement. I have to be sagacious and listen to each party's underlying interest. Often I'll find that I need to sell to one side more than the other and have to find a way to propose my position to them without imposing on them. I'll say something like, "Based on what you're telling me, would you consider..." As is often the case in the Courtroom, this act requires a certain level of diplomacy. I must not give the impression of bias. So my strategy becomes selling to both sides so that the level of persuasion is equal. You'll find that sometimes a situation requires that you slip into a role.

Introversion or extroversion might be more dominant for you, but we are all capable of assuming the characteristics of our opposite type when the situation calls for it. In her book, *Quiet: The Power of Introverts*, Susan Cain notes that adopting a different persona in different scenarios can be exhausting and leave us feeling inauthentic. But Cain notes an important exception. The key to borrowing personality traits that don't come easily to us lies in Professor Brian Little's "Free Trait Theory." The theory contends that we are able to act out of character readily when we are motivated by "Core Personal Projects." If the effort is made because we are working toward something we find meaningful, we will be happy to take on challenges that we might find daunting in relation to a less motivating task. Draw motivation from your client's case and advocate as best as you can for your client's sake. If that means you need to be more assertive, play the role of the extrovert. And if you are worried about being too abrasive and argumentative, put your grandstanding aside and let your more introverted qualities shine by getting off the soapbox and focusing on the facts.

Once you are in Court, the judge has the option to buy either your position or opposing counsel's. Judges have a lot to sort through, including facts, evidence, and the jurisprudence that guides them in their decisions. Your mission is to make it as easy as possible for the judge to give you the judgement you are looking for. Keep your argument clean and factual so that it makes legal sense. You don't want to leave any room for the judge to have any qualms.

Your success in life depends heavily upon your ability to sell to and influence the people around you. So much of life is centered on interactions with people, so it should come as no surprise that our success, our joy, and our fulfilment in life are often determined by our ability to help others change their thoughts, beliefs and actions. This is done by assuming a sales approach to communication. We must endeavour to identify problems and provide solutions to those problems in order to sell a product or idea. Then, once we have demonstrated a reasonable response to a need, we can confidently make a call to action and get the result we desire.

CHAPTER 3

NON-VERBAL COMMUNICATION:

IMPROVING YOUR IMAGE IN THE ROLE OF ADVOCATE

AS A LAWYER YOU must maintain a professional and generally likable demeanor in order to give a favorable impression of your case to the Court. This applies whether presenting to a judge or to a jury. Both audiences have their challenges: while a judge has the task of presenting a verdict that is free of bias with only the law as a guide, a jury is more susceptible to emotional appeals but often views a lawyer with great skepticism. Most people can drastically improve their influence by giving some thought to the way they present themselves.

Start by asking yourself, "What do I communicate about myself when making a first impression?" What does your physical appearance say about you? When people see you, they're going to make judgements about you. Right or wrong, good or bad, moral, immoral, amoral, it doesn't matter; it's a fact of life.

When people see us, they draw conclusions about us. They might not write you off completely, but they might view you as less capable or creditable.

As a lawyer it is important to manage your impression by dressing appropriately. Present yourself well when you come in contact with clients and coworkers, so that rather than detracting from your ability your appearance will bolster it.

> **GUIDELINES FOR DRESSING APPROPRIATELY**
>
> • Generally, those in the legal profession dress more conservatively. Don't reveal too much skin or wear clothing or accessories that might distract your audience from your message.
>
> • Purchase higher quality clothing in classic styles, rather than filling your closet with trendier items.
>
> • Take your suits to a tailor. Ill-fitting clothing can be too revealing or too sloppy; neither makes a good impression.
>
> • Good grooming is also important. Hair should be neat, and (for women) makeup should appear natural and professional.
>
> • Wear shoes that are professional (women should refrain from wearing heels that are too high or attention-pulling) and keep them in good repair.
>
> • Remember that you are representing yourself, your firm, and your clients. Aim to keep your appearance neutral so that all attention is put on your message.

Some of the best things that you can do to improve your ability to influence and persuade other people have to do not with your words but your appearance. And that includes the confidence you project and the sincerity you demonstrate in your eye contact and body language. First impressions speak even before we do. We only get one shot at them.

Think about your non-verbal communication. When speaking to or listening to someone, are you inadvertently communicating that you are bored? People will get that sense if you aren't making an active effort to engage them. Are you giving off the impression that you're angry or detached? Do you come across as condescending? All of these impressions are transmitted through non-verbal communication. If your eyes are rolled back and you're looking around or your arms are crossed, people will pick up on the non-verbal message you're sending. They will not engage with you if you're communicating boredom, anger, condescension, or any other negative attitude.

If you want to manage your non-verbal communication you must become engaged. Pay attention to your posture, the way you hold your hands, the way you sit, and the way you use your eyes. You want to let the other person know, whether you're speaking to them or listening to them, that you are engaged in the conversation, that it is important to you, and that they are important to you. Without this, there can be no persuasive exchange.

> **POSTURES TO AVOID:**
> Arms crossed
> Hands in pockets
> Thumbs in pockets or waistband
> Hands clasped in front of your body or behind your back

Trials require you to manage your demeanor throughout. You will have to take special care not to upset the judge or the jury in a moment of weakness by acting boorishly or aloof. Watch your body language. Treat opposing counsel and the legal process with respect. A lot of lawyers think that they need to be aggressive or even rude to get their point across. But they do themselves a disservice. Consider the popular quote, "Profanity is the effort of a feeble mind to express itself forcefully." In the end, being rude will only make you look foolish. Often lawyers will turn to aggression when they lack confidence in their presentation. Don't let anxiety manifest as aggression. Do away with anxiety instead by being prepared. And know that timidity can be just as problematic, but is resolved in the same way. When a lawyer is too timid and is unable to present an argument confidently, the audience will doubt the soundness of the argument. Adequate preparation will always make you feel more at ease.

Each person must develop his or her own style of public speaking. You will only find the right fit by practicing and getting comfortable with speaking to your audience. I had a professor in law school (who is now a respected judge) who was, for me, the epitome of eloquence. He spoke well and never became flustered. He would walk into class with a black binder in hand, open it, and set it down. Then he would begin to speak, walking away from his podium and never glancing at his notes. Every so often, he would return to the binder and flip the page. At first that gesture baffled me since he had clearly committed his presentation to memory, but I soon realized that the act of turning the page kept him on track. And there is great value in that. Knowing the order of your points and the topics you want to cover helps prevent rambling or hesitation, and in turn helps you deliver an eloquent speech.

Do what you need to do to gain confidence and become comfortable speaking. Spend time recharging before appearing in Court. If you are an introvert, you likely regain your energy through solitude. Once you are satisfied that you are well prepared (see Chapter 8), spend some time alone going over your presentation and practicing presentation elements you might find challenging, such as projecting your voice. Extroverts require social interaction when they need to recharge, so if you get your energy this way you can spend some additional time with a colleague to rehearse your speaking points and to strike the right tone. Make time in your schedule to engage in the tasks that suit your personality. Doing so will give you the confidence to communicate effectively when the need arrives.

When presenting, some people prefer to have a few key points written down to remind them of the order of their argument. Others don't want to lose momentum by referring to notes. To gain confidence in speaking without notes, American criminal defense attorney F. Lee Bailey recommends the following exercise in his book, *To Be A Trial Lawyer*. After developing your outline, write all of the relevant facts and key phrases on separate cards. Shuffle the cards and test your ability to return them to their proper order. This will help you to memorize the flow of your overall argument. When practicing with the cue cards, challenge yourself to recall as much as possible from a quick glance at your notes. Introverts are more likely to prepare extensive speaking notes, and might fall into the trap of reading right from the page when presenting. Know that using notes will create a barrier between you and your audience, so the less you need to refer to them, the better. Bailey goes so far as to say, "Written materials are a crutch," and he recommends that trial lawyers speak without notes if they wish to give their message the greatest advantage. But adequate preparation is essential. Extroverts might speak with confidence extemporaneously, but can truly benefit from the act of preparation that many introverts consider a necessity.

If you remember only one thing it is that respect is fundamental. Address the court and witnesses decorously and be mindful of the way you respond, especially when you object. You are advocating on behalf of your client. So anything you do in bad taste will reflect badly on him or her.

CHAPTER 4

Creating a Dialogue:

Communicating with Your Audience

The first challenge you will face when communicating is getting people to pay attention to you. No worthwhile communication can take place until you gain the complete attention of your audience, and the moment you lose that attention, effective communication stops. Talking when nobody is listening will get you nowhere. The number one secret to earning and maintaining your listener's attention is to create a dialogue by getting them involved. If you want someone's attention, be attentive to the concerns or interests of that person.

In other words, don't just talk to your audience, talk with your audience. This advice may not always apply in a Courtroom setting, as there are distinct rules to follow, but is especially helpful when engaging with clients and coworkers. Watch body language for signs of engagement, such as eye contact and nodding. Maintain an exchange of ideas, feelings and thoughts. Unless we have dialogue, we are not communicating. Dialogue gives people a reason to pay attention because they are involved in the communication process. Their thoughts and feelings become part of the speaker's presentation. When the audience feels a connection to what the speaker is saying then the speaker has achieved effective communication. One way to interact with your audience when your listener is unlikely to speak directly (as is the case with a judge or jury) is to address expected questions and concerns on behalf of the audience as you outline your argument. Using questions can also help you to re-establish contact when you feel you have lost your audience's attention.

Active Listening

Real communication doesn't operate in only one direction. The best communicators are active listeners. Realistically, it is common to find that when someone else is talking, most people aren't processing the information that's being shared and trying to internalize it. Instead, they're concentrating on how they intend to respond and waiting for somebody to take a breath so they can jump in and add their perspective. Both introverts and extroverts can be guilty of committing this social taboo, though they are motivated by different reasons. Introverts commonly mull over what they are going to say when engaging in a dialogue, which makes it easy to miss what their conversation partner is saying. Extroverts might monopolize a conversation because they prefer talking rather than listening. Regardless of the reason, you must make every effort to be attentive and process what others are saying. It's an essential skill for lawyers, whether dealing with clients, with opposing counsel, or with judges.

- **GIVE THE SPEAKER YOUR FULL ATTENTION.**

Maintain eye contact (3-5 seconds per person is ideal). This is not the time to leaf through your notes. When you are distracted, your speaker will be offended and find your behaviour disrespectful. It is much harder to persuade someone you have already offended. Don't make things harder for yourself by being disrespectful.

To gain confidence in making group eye contact, practice redirecting your gaze in a less formal group, perhaps of colleagues or friends, so that the habit will come to feel natural to you and you won't become distracted and lose track of your thoughts when trying to address a group in Court.

- **DON'T INTERRUPT.**

One of Dr. Richard's findings in assessing lawyers' personality traits was that lawyers tend to exhibit a greater sense of urgency. He notes that this can be great for clients, as their cases are moved along expeditiously, but this trait also makes lawyers prone to interrupting others. Let the speaker articulate his or her thoughts.

- **USE BODY LANGUAGE TO SIGNAL YOUR INTEREST.**

Position yourself so that you are facing the speaker. Nod when you agree or understand. Make comments when appropriate.

- **DEMONSTRATE YOUR UNDERSTANDING.**
When you ask a question or make a response, recall details and summarize the speaker's key point to ensure that you understand. Additionally, try to structure your argument to meet their needs.

Pay attention to what your audience values. Is the judge looking for a precedent that matches your case as closely as possible? Does a jury need to be able to visualize your client's difficulty? Give them what they want. These are often details you would be sharing anyway, but you can emphasize the points that will reassure your audience that they will be making the right choice if they give you the judgement you're after. Not only will listening actively help you connect with your audience, but training your ear will also help you catch statements made by opposing counsel that can help you strengthen your argument in presenting your client's case.

Another key to maintaining your listener's attention is making a personal connection. Getting and keeping others' attention has become a major challenge. Sociologists are calling this the most disconnected generation. They speak of a loss of intimacy and an increase in feelings of alienation and isolation. That makes establishing rapport and building deep, meaningful relationships a major accomplishment. Listening actively is the key to making those connections.

We must gain a listener's attention by being interesting as well as by being interested. Discover what appeals to your audience, then zero in on that interest and build your presentation around it. Messages become interesting to us and gain our attention only when they become personal – only when we can relate them to our own experiences. Think about which news stories attract your attention. There's a good chance they appeal to you because you connect to them on a personal level.

Creating a genuine connection by taking an interest in your audience will boost your ability to communicate with others. I believe that there are two kinds of people in this world. There's the kind of person who walks into a room and says, "Here I am," and then there's the type who walks in and says, "Ah, there you are." If we want to earn our listener's attention, we need to be the kind of people who say, "There you are." As the saying goes: "It takes two minutes to make a friend if you talk about them, but it takes two weeks to make a friend if you talk about yourself."

So, once you have gained your audience's approval and attention, how can you maintain it? There are six very effective tactics that you can use.

Six Tactics for Keeping Your Audience's Attention

1. Organize your thoughts before you begin speaking.

This is something introverts might do naturally but that extroverts – who often share their thoughts aloud as they occur – might struggle with. The most common source of confusing messages is muddled thinking. If a thought isn't clear in our minds, it's going to sound worse when we share it aloud. People don't want to struggle to understand. Most will quit listening if our message doesn't make sense because our thoughts aren't organized.

2. Get right to the point.

One of the most effective ways to lose an audience is to leave them thinking, "So, what's the point?" Give your listeners the meat of your story or presentation to chew on while you elaborate with details.

3. Translate what you have to say into benefits for your listener.

People will seldom ignore what you're saying if they believe there's something in it for them. Remember, people are always tuned into station WIIFM: What's In It For Me?

4. Ask questions to involve the listener.

When you're speaking, don't be afraid to ask questions to learn what interests members of your audience. Ask questions as you make your points to make sure your listeners are with you, and give them the opportunity to contribute to the conversation. Remember, your goal is to carry on a dialogue, not a monologue. Look for feedback in your listeners' body language.

5. Be genuine.

Don't be afraid to let the real you shine through. Our attempts at communication are weakened when we try to say things in ways that are unnatural to us because we have to take on the additional role of acting, and most of us are better at communicating than we are at acting. You won't benefit from acting much more formal or much more casual than you are naturally. The former can cause you to feel anxious and make errors, while the latter can make you seem aloof rather than approachable. Instead of trying to copy someone else's style, concentrate on what you are saying and on the audience you are speaking to. Let the real you come through and you'll be more convincing and more comfortable.

6. Be enthusiastic.

If you're not excited about your subject or discussion, how can you expect your listeners to be very interested? Identify the most interesting features of your case and communicate them enthusiastically. Be animated. Be lively. Move around. Gesticulate. If you put a little enthusiasm into your dialogue, you'll have a much greater impact on your listeners than if you drone on listlessly.

Getting a listener's attention can be one of the most challenging and rewarding aspects of communicating with others. But it isn't as difficult as it may at first appear. You can get attention without pulling stunts. Make the effort to connect to your audience. Then, maintain that connection. This can be accomplished by getting your listeners involved even if you do so by using rhetorical questions, encouraging your audience to provide the answers.

CHAPTER 5

Dynamic Descriptions:

Connecting to Your Audience Through Storytelling

The esteemed American criminal defense attorney, F. Lee Bailey, shared in his book *To Be a Trial Lawyer* that those who wish to be good lawyers must have a superior command of language. I'd take that a step further and say they have to be good storytellers. You must endeavour to deliver a story that is clear and concise, yet comprehensive. When performing to persuade in Court you must obviously have a factually and legally solid case. But often a jury will not act purely on reason. People make decisions, in part, based on how they feel. Telling a compelling story can make the difference between winning and losing a close case. Good stories that are interesting, memorable, and illustrate a message can inspire, motivate, teach, and persuade.

How many absolutely compelling, life-changing, career-building, sales-inducing, Court-swaying presentations have you heard, or even given? I guarantee if you've heard a Court submission, a speech, sermon or sales presentation that you enjoyed, you'll remember at least part of what made it so memorable was the story shared. When sharing stories as part of a presentation, your audience must find them interesting, have an emotional connection to them, and find a lesson to be learned from them. Most importantly, your story must have an obvious connection to the point of your oral submission, speech or conversation.

It is commonly accepted that a story fulfils a profound human need to grasp the patterns of living, not merely on an intellectual level, but also on a personal and emotional level. When you speak to an audience, whether it is an audience of one or one thousand, a judge or a jury, you are setting up a conversation between *your* voice and *their* minds and hearts. This is why a good keynote speech has rich and well-developed stories. When we teach and explain the complex, a good story or metaphor is effective because the audience can better form an image of what you are saying and place themselves inside the story to understand the perspective being shared.

It's also worth noting that telling a story will win over your audience better than a lecture or argument will. Without a doubt, stories provide the best way to emotionally connect with your audience. Your listeners may not recall everything you share, but a well-told story will stick with them.

Story Telling Basics

• Stories should be your own, or your client's. Sharing a story that includes personal experience will make it more heartfelt and interesting. If you tell a story that belongs to the world, most people will already have heard it and you will lose attention and credibility. If your audience has heard it before, your entire presentation will come across as cliché and will be less convincing because it will seem that you have plucked details from other stories in order to make the case more compelling.

• Stories should be true. When sharing a metaphor, a story can be embellished or exaggerated for artistic effect. You can even combine a couple of anecdotes; or use funnier names. However, when you are presenting a case, your stories must be grounded in facts.

• When sharing a story, your protagonist needn't always be the hero. A heroic protagonist can create a barrier to connection, and your audience won't feel inspired or sympathetic. People are drawn to stories about real people. If you construct a hero figure, listeners might not be as moved by his tale. To incorporate real people's perspectives, you can try varying the perspectives you share and your protagonist's role in the stories you tell. For example, your protagonist might have witnessed an event and learned from others.

• Don't be afraid to share stories, even in unconventional storytelling situations. Some presentations may require numbers and statistics, but these too can be made to be interesting. I like to say, "Numbers do not have to be numbing." Don't make the common mistake of reading from slides. Use your statistics and numbers in a story. With jurisprudence, the same principles apply. Every lawyer knows that legal principles are found in established case-law, and the known applications and interpretation of relevant pieces of legislation or procedural rules guide the Court in its ruling. Use what you know, and keep it interesting. Wrap your key points and established principles into a story.

• When sharing stories, aim to convey variety and extremes. Try keeping records of your experiences in lists organized by subject. Look at good experiences and bad experiences. Focus on the superlatives: the best, the worst, the biggest, the smallest, the most successful, the biggest failure. These details can make stories more exciting.

• It can be helpful, when relating an event, to share it in present tense to help your listeners experience what you are sharing. Instead of "then X happened," try, "Now X happens." Also use the active voice, rather than the passive. Say "X did Y to Z," instead of "Y was done to Z by X."

• Being a good storyteller doesn't require grand theatrics – in fact, overacting can hurt the integrity of a story. Being a good storyteller means being personable and straight-forward. Focus on sharing relevant details in an honest way and get your listeners to imagine themselves in your protagonist's shoes.

• Use pauses and stillness for impact. When you deliver your story, or your oral submission, don't distract your audience with unnecessary movement. And when it comes to the key point of your story, stand still. Do not distract from the point. Your listeners will rely on verbal punctuation to identify important information, so your stillness will signal to the Court, your audience, that this is what they should be writing down. When you do move, move with purpose. Aim to gesticulate on a phrase that indicates movement. Consider the logical moments to move. Be aware of phrases that relate to movement. If, for example, you are saying, "She was so startled, she froze," it's logical that you wouldn't move when you're talking about standing still.

• Make it easier for your audience to recognize key points by selecting key words that have punch. Remember that words pack more meaning than their dictionary definition. Two words might mean the same thing, but one might carry more emotional impact. Consider accident vs. collision. The denotation (explicit meaning) might be similar, but the connotation (associated meaning) gives the word "accident" less impact than "collision" because we commonly describe minor fender benders as accidents and more dangerous crashes as collisions.

• Remember that all of your communication has an aim, even your stories. Include a call for action with your stories so your audience will know what is needed from them.

• Pepper your language with rhetorical devices that add force to your words.

USEFUL RHETORICAL DEVICES TO KNOW AND PUT INTO PRACTICE

Amplification: Expanding a simple statement, often by adding detail or expanding on a story or idea.

Anaphora: Repetition of the same word at the beginning of successive clauses.

Asyndeton: The omission of conjunctions between words, phrases, or clauses.

Antithesis: Juxtaposition of contrasting ideas or phrases.

Catachresis: An extravagant, unexpected, or far-fetched metaphor.

Copia: An abundance of expression.

Decorum: Dictates that the style should suit the subject, audience, speaker, and occasion.

Ellipsis: Omission of one or more words, intending the audience to supply them.

Enargeria: Vivid description, which re-creates something or someone before the eyes.

Enthymeme: Part of the argument is left unstated because it is assumed to be true. (Implied)

Hyperbole: Exaggeration used for emphasis.

Isocolon: Phrases of commensurate length and similar structure.

Macrologia: Long-winded speech. (To be avoided)

Metonymy: Naming a thing or concept by something closely associated with it.

Paradiastole: A kind of euphemism. Substituting a negative term for a term with positive associations.

Paranomasia: Playing on the sounds and meanings of words. (Puns)

CHAPTER 6

PRESENTATION ELEMENTS:

PRESENTING TO A JURY

WHEN PRESENTING TO A jury, your aim will be to get the jury caught up in the drama of the case and to see things from your client's perspective. As an advocate speaking on your client's behalf, it is your duty to encourage the jury to be receptive to your arguments. When speaking, try speaking directly to a juror in the back row. This will make it easier to find the appropriate voice level and will make your address more intimate.

OPENING STATEMENT

Right from the beginning, when you make your opening statement, you will be establishing a rapport with the jury. This is when presenting yourself, and by extension your client, as someone with character will be beneficial. If you start off strong, your message will stick and the jury will consider your perspective throughout the trial. Keeping your client's perspective top of mind for the jury offers you an incredible advantage, as the jury might be more skeptical when witnesses make statements against your client. So, in your opening statement present your case with conviction to get the jury on side. The members of the jury will want to deliver a fair judgement, so make it easy for them to come to your desired conclusion; keep your delivery simple, with enough details to keep your client's story interesting. Your desired outcome should be clear and logical to the jury.

Suggested structure for an opening statement:

a) Introduce yourself and your client
b) Explain the opening statement's function
c) State the focus of your case
d) Set the scene and share your client's story
e) List the evidence that will be shared with the jury
f) Explain any major exhibits
g) Expound your desired verdict

Once again, the jury will be judging your character. You won't want to do anything that will hurt your credibility. This is why it's important not to make claims that are too strong in your opening statement. The jury will lose trust in you if you overpromise and under-deliver. Don't guarantee an exact testimony; give the jury an idea of what they can expect to hear in support of your client's case. This way, if the witness' statement is not exactly what you expected, you will not have tarnished your reputation. And if the witness delivers what you hope, the statement will only reinforce the expectation you shared in your opening statement. Similarly, avoid presenting evidence that might come into question (for example, if a confession was made under great duress). Bring up any concerns you have in a conference in chambers and in a chambers ruling ask that a Court reporter record it so you will have the opportunity to appeal.

Of course, not every piece of evidence will work in your client's favour. In your opening, you also have the opportunity to address any perceived weaknesses. This will allow you to present weaknesses in the best light.

Closing Argument

After the trial has run its course you will have one final opportunity to present your client's case to the jury in order to allow the jury to perform its duty. This is the opportune time to put your storytelling skills to work! Review the rhetorical devices listed in Chapter 5. Use visual aids where possible, or recall key evidence in visual terms as these elements will be more memorable.

In relation to presenting a persuasive closing argument, I'd like to draw your attention to Aristotle's three components of effective persuasion from his writing, *The Rhetoric*. When you break it down, there are three elements: logos, pathos, and ethos. Logos is logic, pathos is passion, and ethos is ethics. If you want to be persuasive, you have to involve all three parts in your presentation. We've already discussed character, which fulfils the ethical component, for which the aim is to build trust. So let's pay attention to the other two: logos and pathos.

Logos: being logical, clear, concise, rational.

Communicate in a clear, concise manner so that your audience will follow your argument. At the end of your presentation you want people to understand your reasoning and come to your desired conclusion.

Pathos: being passionate, moving your listeners, calling upon emotion.

Communicate your belief in your case and be expressive when delivering your message. Speak with your eyes and hands and determine the appropriate tone and pacing. Passion is contagious so it behooves you to employ it in your arguments.

Of course, an effective argument won't have passion without logic, but neither will a strong presentation rely on logic alone. A merely informative presentation has no sense of urgency – no strong call to action. Logic and passion, when paired, make for a powerful presentation. And perfection is achieved when logic and passion are delivered by a person of good character. All three elements together will ensure that an audience trusts, understands, and cares about the message being delivered.

You'll want to include all of the pertinent details, without rambling on. With practice you will find a balance. You will learn how much knowledge of the law you can assume the average person has and how many points from the case should be repeated to drive home your argument. It helps to limit yourself to using only details that are relevant to your desired outcome. Share key points and explain why they are relevant and important. If you have prepared and know exactly what you wish to say, you will find that clarity and brevity naturally occur as you will have removed any redundancies.

Plan out your argument and structure it so that the details you share follow logically from your statements. Again, your job is to make the jury's decision as easy as possible. State why your client's side is credible and why your opponent's side is not. Remind the jury of evidence that supports those statements.

Certainly, the best argument will have the advantage of strong evidence, unarguable law, and a persuasive presentation. A weak case will not likely get you the judgement you are hoping for. But a powerful presentation can help you win a close case.

CHAPTER 7

Organizing Your Argument:

The Mechanics of Effective Submissions

While I don't claim to be the expert on submissions, I have learned a thing or two in the course of my career that I hope I can share with you, and I want to begin by providing you with some principles.

1. Understand the difference between public speaking and powerful oral submissions. A skillful submission is not the same as public speaking. In a public speaking environment, your main goal is to entertain, but in powerful submissions, your goal is to deliver a message your audience needs. Public speaking focuses on the speaker's objective, while oral submissions focus on what the audience, judge and/or jury want.

2. Remember that people, even learned judges, can become overwhelmed and may have very short attention spans. Only provide the information they need to be persuaded. It's estimated that the average North American receives 2,500 messages a day, and desk professionals spend an average of 43% of their time in meetings, on the phone, and in e-mail. Your listeners want to be able to identify your key points just as they might scan an email for the pertinent details. You don't have to tell the Court everything you know, just what's most relevant.

3. Know that your main purpose in every submission is to persuade. Your aim is to get your audience to change its thought process vis-a-vis your client, to take away your message and act in your client's favour. Present what they need to hear to be persuaded to accept your message.

Preparation

Effective submissions are not written speeches. In preparing effective oral submissions begin by asking questions. Then pull out the answers, polish up the language, and organize your work into the correct structure. Focus on your audience's needs and wants. Your audience needs to know:

- What do you know?
- How do you know it?
- Why should they care?
- What do you want them to do about it?

This is something lawyers can do well,

regardless of their personality traits. Introverts are most comfortable analyzing and interpreting events and activities, while extroverts are happier jumping in and experiencing them firsthand. This means introverts often excel in tasks that require research, strategy, and written communication. Conversely, extroverts do well engaging with new people and exchanging ideas.

You have only a short length of time to persuade your audience. Ideally you would understand your audience's needs and motivations completely in order to cater your presentation to your listener, but that is virtually impossible when making oral submissions in Court. The next best thing you can do is arrive prepared.

Think back to the composition or the five paragraph essay you wrote in high school. Your case will often follow that blueprint. The order of your information should be systematic and rehearsed. When you give your opening address, present all of the information the Court can expect to hear. Then, the body of your argument will present your evidence. Finally, your closing will serve as a summary and will be your last opportunity to present your case in a way that is compelling and clear.

I've always said, just as with performances, there are only three types of submissions: the one you plan to give, the one you gave, and the one you wish you had given. In preparing for an effective submission, when you are getting ready to go out and give this powerful speech, there are a few things you will need to keep in mind. In order to deliver the submission you want to give, you will need to follow five steps.

1. DEVELOP YOUR OBJECTIVE.

Put simply, what are you trying to accomplish? What do you ultimately want your audience to do? What kind of reaction do you want to get from the audience as a result of your time with them? It can be useful to begin with a theory for your case (fairness, justice, gender equality, freedom under law, etc.) Establishing a case's theory when assembling your information can help you get into the right mindset and can inform the way you interact with others during the process. Knowing where you stand, and why, will determine how you communicate with council, what language you use when you draft a claim or defence, and what tone you will take in your position. All of this will help you argue for your primary objective.

2. DETERMINE THE MAIN POINTS FOR THE BODY OF YOUR TALK.

The main points must directly support the theory of your case. I'd recommend no more than three (a maximum of five) main points. Identify the key points that the Court must understand if your submission objective is to be met. Which ones will best lead to your objective? What ideas do you most want your audience to remember? Do your main points clearly support the theory of your case?

3. DEVELOP YOUR OPENING.

While I would not recommend you memorize your entire submission, as doing so could leave you nervous and flustered, I do recommend you memorize your opening, your closing, and your transitional statements.

You can use note cards for the main body of your submission, if you need to. Index cards work well. Write some keywords that will trigger the next three minutes of the story you're going to tell. Bullet points should be no longer than seven words and should not be full sentences. Otherwise you will be tempted to read exactly what is written, hurting your credibility. Look down, scan your first cue, and let that evoke a complete idea. Then speak. When you finish that thought, look down, scan the next cue, think, and speak. Generally, most audiences will be very accepting of notes.

However, when delivering an opening, the purpose is to capture the Court's attention and keep it. Listeners will form an opinion of you within the first few minutes and you want to encourage them to listen to you, allowing you to introduce the subject of your submission in the best light and establish your credibility. Start off with something attention-grabbing: a fact, a statistic, maybe even a powerful "humanizing" statement about your client.

4. Memorize your transition statements.
Transitions are like segues. These links join the end of one point to the beginning of the next, and they should be seamless. Often just a phrase that signals you are wrapping up one section and beginning another will suffice: "Now that we understand the importance of A-B-C, let's

shift over to X-Y-Z," or "In addition to this, ..." Whichever transitions you choose, they should link your points together smoothly so you don't appear to be jumping around unsure of what you will talk about next. Transitions contribute to a polished presentation.

5. Polish your closing.

Your closing should review the purpose of the submission, summarize the key points, and end with a call to action. Leave your audience with something to make them think. Ask for the result – the judgment – that you believe your client is entitled to.

THINGS TO AVOID WHEN CLOSING:

• Don't ramble. Once you've said, "In closing," don't carry on and on. If you string out your close, the Court, and generally any audience, will become impatient.

• Don't stop abruptly. I've seen lawyers essentially say, "Well, that's it." Instead, deliver a summary of the key points and a little story. Wrap things up in a neat package and put a bow on the top.

• Don't admit you goofed. If you've left something out, it's possible the judge or jury didn't realize. If you forgot something, you're welcome to include it at the end, but don't call attention to your mistake and berate yourself for being a bad speaker, or an incompetent lawyer. You wouldn't want to convince your audience of your ineptness and lose your power to persuade as a result.

• Don't suddenly change your delivery style. If you have been a fairly serious, technical speaker, don't suddenly speed up and become energetic in your delivery. You don't want to confuse or distract your audience.

CHAPTER 8

THE FEAR FACTOR:

OVERCOMING PUBLIC SPEAKING ANXIETY

How many times have you heard someone say, "Hey, we're all nervous about giving speeches. No big deal. All you have to do when you get up there is picture the audience naked"? We've all heard that line over and over again. The irony of it is that the reason so many of us get nervous is because, as we are facing an audience, we feel naked ourselves. We feel vulnerable and exposed, and we get the feeling that we are moments away from the audience spotting all of our shortcomings.

Unfortunately, if you do not know how to manage your anxiety, you might make a bad impression either by being too aggressive or too timid. Extroverts can sometimes get in trouble due to their tendency to speak without first planning their speech. Many extroverted people working in the legal profession who are anxious about presenting believe that the practice of law thrives on conflict. When this false belief is paired with their natural ability to think through problems aloud and their preference for sharing thoughts as they occur, they can come across as confrontational. Dr. Richard's research has found that lawyers are more defensive and sensitive to criticism than the general population, so this is a common problem. Aggression seems to me to be something people turn to when they are nervous or ill-prepared and hope to intimidate opposing council or to win their verdict through force. Do not make this mistake.

Timidity is just as hindering, and is often how anxiety manifests in introverts. If you want your message to be well-voiced, you must speak it with conviction. If you stumble your way through a presentation to the Court, you will not be doing your client any favours. This is especially important when presenting to a jury, in which case your demeanour, tone of voice, and body language will have a greater impact. A jury will be less likely to believe your statements if they are spoken with hesitation. But it is also important not to let your nerves upset your delivery when presenting to a judge. A judge will not be as persuaded by your argument if it is not given clearly.

But there's good news. Stage fright is purely a state of mind, and can be overcome. The subconscious does not have the ability to negate information. Whatever it is you're feeding your brain, the subconscious will affirm. So you'll need to change your thinking.

The following are five tips for better managing

your stage fright and making your anxiety work for you. I advise you not to just read all five tips and pick the one you think is going to work best for you. You will see the greatest results if you employ each one of these five tips. And the more nervous you get when you're delivering a presentation, or as you're preparing for a major submission, the more critical it is that you use all five.

1. **RE-LABEL THE EXPERIENCE.**

    Instead of understanding public speaking as a negative thing, try to view it, and embrace it, as something positive. When you experience physiological symptoms, such as shaky hands or dry mouth, recognize that your body is pumped full of adrenaline which can give you the power to deliver something great. Professional athletes revel in the moments just before the game because they know that they're getting the extra bit of juice they need to give them a competitive edge. Experienced speakers also think of adrenaline and nerves as a booster shot of sorts. So, when you've got adrenaline coursing through your body, take comfort in knowing that your body is getting you physically, emotionally, and mentally ready to take on the challenge you're facing. You are in your ready mode, and that's exactly where you want to be.

2. **SPEAK POSITIVELY.**

    The subconscious does not have the ability to negate information, so use that to your advantage and speak only in the affirmative about the experience you're about to have. If you hear yourself saying something negative like, "I am so scared," change that language right away.

Don't think, "I'm scared," but "I'm excited," "I'm pumped," or, "I'm jacked."

Don't get caught up thinking, "This is going to be awful. I'm going to go blank in the middle of my talk or someone will ask me a question I won't have the answer to and people will find out I'm not as smart as I pretend to be." Instead, think, "I'm going to do a great job. This is the presentation that's really going to get people respecting me."

And while you're at it, delete the phrase "have to" from your vocabulary. From this point forward, make the commitment to yourself to say "get to" in its place. Embrace the opportunity and you will feel the difference. Automatically, you will find yourself in a very different emotional state.

3. COME UP WITH A PERSONAL MANTRA THAT RESONATES FOR YOU.

A mantra is a one-line statement that fills you up from the inside out and puts you into the right mental, emotional, and physical state. It puts you into the zone.

For example, watching an interview with the famous basketball player, Michael Jordan, I learned that he would recite the same mantra before major games, saying, "This is what I do, this is who I am." Come up with your own mantra and use it to build your confidence before a presentation.

4. VISUALIZE.

We have all heard so much about the power of

visualization. Don't be skeptical. It works! Create in your mind a clear picture of what will be your surroundings when you stand in front of a judge or jury. Imagine the sound of your voice as you deliver a strong presentation. Think about how you're standing and get a sense of where everyone in the Courtroom is and how many people are there. Picture what they look like. Create as realistic a visualization as possible.

It's not just about coming up with that mental image. In order for the visualization process to work, you have to get in touch with the emotion behind the vision. So, as you create that visual image, think about how you are feeling. As you're speaking your opening words, imagine the audience responding by sitting up straighter, and leaning in towards you. Think about how affirming that feels. Get in touch with the emotion. The stronger the emotion, the greater the chance that you will experience the success you're imagining because your mind will believe you have already performed the task with confidence.

5. **Practice.**
Here's an old joke. What's the quickest way to Carnegie Hall? You know the answer: practice, practice, practice. And you know why it's been around for so long? Because there is a lot of truth to it. You won't become a master of any craft overnight. You have to work at it; you have to be willing to roll up your sleeves. You can't just try something a few times; you have to repeat it over and over and over again. In his bestselling book *Outliers*, author Malcolm Gladwell introduced and explained the 10,000 hour rule. Gladwell stated

that in order to achieve great success at anything one must practice for at least 10,000 hours. For example, The Beatles played gigs in Germany for years before the world was turned on to the "British explosion."

As the well-known actor Michael Cain said, "Rehearsal is the work. Performance is the relaxation." A good presentation doesn't come about by accident. Practice in front of real people. Try recording yourself to hear how your message comes across. An audio recording is helpful, but video is better. Analyze the recording to identify mannerisms you'd like to include or remove, and take note of the overall impression you make.

Practice is a structured event, and the emphasis is on improving and preparing the relevant skills one needs to perform. Dedicated practice enables you to identify your weaknesses and focus on improving them before worrying about your overall delivery. Spend some time on whatever you find most challenging, whether it be building rapport, transitioning from one point to the next, or becoming comfortable with a more eloquent vocabulary. Push yourself to achieve more. As Reverend Al Sharpton shared in *The Rejected Stone: Al Sharpton and the Path to American Leadership,* when he accompanied Muhammad Ali on a training run Ali only started timing the run after circling the track twice. The 'track' Ali had selected was the Central Park reservoir – a lake encircled by a one-and-a-half-mile path. When Sharpton asked why he hadn't started the timer before they'd begun their three-mile run, Ali responded, "I train myself to start timing after

I'm tired."

Once you have practiced you will be ready to rehearse. Rehearsal is the summoning of skills and strategies into performance mode. Rehearse answers to potential questions. Collect at least three people who have a working knowledge of your case, or the relevant area of law, to act as your audience and pose questions. Oftentimes you can make or break a presentation during the question and answer period. But if you prepare and practice you will be so much more at ease.

If you employ planned practice and comprehensive rehearsal, when you get to Court it will feel like déjà vu. You will have been here before, you will have done this before, and you will see the positive outcome coming your way.

Before You Present

To get into a more relaxed mindset there are three types of strategies that you can use to calm yourself down: physical, psychological, and behavioural.

Physical strategies:
- Practice deep breathing. Immediately before you begin, breathe in through your nose slowly to the count of five, and then breathe out through your mouth to the count of five. This will help slow your heart rate, relieving some tension in your body.

- Try some isometric exercises to get rid of excess nervousness. Push the palms of your hands together firmly for a count of ten. Release and repeat. Tense various muscle groups and then relax them: tense your legs and relax them, tense your biceps, your fists, etc. Do some gentle head nods and roll your neck slightly to relax your neck muscles.

- Exercising several hours before your submission can also help mitigate anxiety. A regular exercise program will reduce that feeling of breathlessness you might get while you speak and will provide you with greater stamina.

- Make eye contact with the judge and or the jury. It might sound intimidating, but doing so will actually help to put you at ease. When a speaker looks at someone in the audience and smiles, the person smiles back. Don't just pretend there isn't anyone around you. Look at the people in the room; have a conversation with them and you will feel more at ease.

PSYCHOLOGICAL STRATEGIES:

- Acknowledge your anxiety and turn your mind to positive thoughts. Say to yourself, "I'm a little anxious about this submission right now, but that's okay; I'm just excited. It's all going to be fine."

- Look for the silver lining. We tend to worry about worst case scenarios: "What if I forget one of the facts, or forget to mention an important element of the case?" Instead, iterate positive affirmations: "I am prepared. I know what I'm talking about."

- Visualize. Create a mental picture of yourself performing in Court at your most confident, eloquent, compelling, and successful.

BEHAVIOURAL STRATEGIES:
- Practice, practice, practice. Rehearse your submission several times before attempting to deliver it live. Get your colleagues to listen, if you have to. Record yourself and learn from the recording.

- Speak at every opportunity in order to get comfortable with the content. With each experience you will improve your speaking skills.

- Take note of your presentation's strong and weak points. Keep what works and toss what doesn't.

- And before you begin, avoid excessive amounts of caffeine. You don't want to be completely wired, as it can be off-putting to your audience.

These physical, psychological or behavioural strategies will help you steady your nerves so that you will be ready to conquer the Courtroom.

CHAPTER 9

Your Reaction Matters:

Receiving the Verdict

There will come times when the product you're selling simply isn't that good. In these cases you will have an uphill battle. Try to focus on the value of the experience whether you win or lose. Each experience is an opportunity to practice your newfound skills and to perfect your communication style. In one such situation, after I lost at the Court of Appeal I was actually complimented by the Court; even though the product I was representing was substandard, I could take pride in the fact that I did a good job of selling my case.

You can only present the strongest case possible and sometimes that isn't going to give you the win. That's just reality. Sometimes the jurisprudence doesn't work in your favor. Remember, no single client can make your career but one *can* break your career. So focus on maintaining your integrity. If you lose, make sure that you lose based on the evidence and the facts, not your delivery. And don't take a loss personally. If you were the best advocate you could be for your client, then it will have been the case that lost, not you.

Try to handle the verdict with grace whether you win or lose. This is something extroverts might need to remind themselves of. Extroverts benefit greatly from the excitement they feel from external stimulation. It motivates them to take on challenges and take risks. But while throwing one's self into a project has the potential to lead to great highs it can also bring with it crushing lows. Take wins and losses in stride. A verdict given in your favor does not always warrant celebration and boastfulness. If you think about it, winning is just the natural result of a strong case and good advocacy. In other words, that's what is supposed to happen. And opposing counsel will recognize that your case was simply stronger. There's no need to insult your opponent. After all, we're all doing what we can to represent our clients fairly.

Afterword

My goal in writing this book was to provide professionals – particularly lawyers – with a concise public speaking guide for easy reference. The necessary skills and the development of them are informed by personality theory, specifically introversion and extroversion.

I believe anyone can be an effective communicator and eloquent advocate. Public speaking is merely a projection of who you are. No matter the personal challenge or hurdle that may exist at the outset, an understanding of your unique personality type and the rigorous development of useful skills will allow you to present your messages (your submissions) in a powerful, eloquent way.

Despite the common platitude that asserts that, besides death, public speaking is the greatest fear, speaking publicly is much more manageable – and even enjoyable – than most believe. It is really only a conversation. If you think about it, whenever you speak outside of your home you are speaking in public. And surely there is no fear in speaking at the grocery store, at the cleaner's, or with friends. On a daily basis we all have multiple conversations, both one-on-one and in small groups. Public speaking is an extension of these everyday conversations. So, while knowing your personality type and understanding how it informs your mastery of everyday conversation is the starting point, whether you identify as an introvert or an extrovert, it's essential that you be true to yourself. This book is meant to provide guidance in honing your craft as an eloquent advocate and effective communicator, but remember that you'll be your most effective if you are true to yourself because the authentic person is the person that the audience, the Court, the judge or jury is going to relate to best.

No matter how shy and reserved or gregarious a person is, he or she can blossom as an eloquent advocate. But make no mistake about it: success requires the technical understanding of selling, storytelling, language usage, and overcoming fear and anxiety. Furthermore, it requires practice. The first step is to simply get started.

As one of my absolute favourite professional public speakers, Les Brown, says: "You don't have to be great to get started, but you have to get started to be great."

Sources

Alter, Cara Hale. The Credibility Code: How to Project Confidence & Competence When It Matters Most. S.l.: Meritus, 2012. Print.

Aristotle. Rhetoric. Ed. W. Rhys Roberts. Mineola, NY: Dover Publications, 2004. Print.

Bailey, F. Lee. To Be a Trial Lawyer. New York: J. Wiley, 1994. Print.

Cain, Susan. Quiet: The Power of Introverts in a World That Can't Stop Talking. New York: Crown, 2012. Print.

Gladwell, Malcolm. Outliers: The Story of Success. New York: Back Bay Books, 2011. Print.

Hegland, Kenney F. Trial and Practice Skills in a Nutshell. St. Paul: West Pub., 1978. Print.

Jung, C. G. Psychological Types. Princeton, NJ: Princeton UP, 1976. Print.

Maxey, Cyndi, and Kevin E. O'Connor. Present like a Pro: The Field Guide to Mastering the Art of Business, Professional, and Public Speaking. New York: St. Martin's Griffin, 2006. Print.

Nardi, Dario. "Neuroscience of Personality: Principles of the Psyche." Lecture.

Richard, Larry. "A Breed Apart?." The American Lawyer. N.p., n.d. Web. 1 Sept. 2013. <http://www.americanlawyer.com/id=1202497964562/A-Breed-Apart?slreturn=20140224073517>.

Richard, Larry. "Coaching Transformational Leaders with the Myers-Briggs Assessment."

Richard, Larry. "Herding Cats: The Lawyer Personality Revealed." Docstoc.com. Managing Partner Forum, 24 Aug. 2011.

Web. Fall 2013. <http://www.docstoc.com/docs/91794264/HERDING-CATS-The-Lawyers-Personality-Revealed>.

Richard, Larry. "How Your Personality Affects Your Practice- The Lawyer Types." A.B.A. Journal (July 1993): 74-79.

Sharpton, Al. The Rejected Stone: Al Sharpton and the Path to American Leadership. United States: Massenburg Media, 2013. Print.

Shaub, Joseph. "Lawyers and Their Psychological Types." Http://josephshaub.com/. N.p., 2010. Web. Fall 2013. <http://josephshaub.com/pdfs/sfl_oa16.pdf>.

Sjodin, Terri L. SALESpeak: Everybody Sells Something. Waco, TX: WRS Pub., 1995. Print.

Sommers, Richard J.. Ed. Franklin R. Moskoff. Advocacy in court: a tribute to Arthur Maloney, Q.C."The Opening Statement and Closing Argument to the Jury in a Civil Case." Toronto, Ont.: Canada Law Book, 1986. 163-169. Print.

Weston, Anthony. A Rulebook for Arguments. Indianapolis: Hackett Pub., 2000. Print.

White, Robert B. The Art of Trial. Aurora, Ont.: Canada Law Book, 1993. Print.

www.ingramcontent.com/pod-product-compliance
Lightning Source LLC
Chambersburg PA
CBHW072103290426
44110CB00014B/1806